BEAUTY AND THE BEAST

A Basic Pantomime in Three Acts

by

TRUDY WEST

WILTSHIRE LIBRARY & MUSEUM SERVICE

SAMUEL FRENCH

LONDON
NEW YORK TORONTO SYDNEY HOLLYWOOD

COPYRIGHT 1953 BY SAMUEL FRENCH LTD

This play is fully protected under the copyright laws of the British Commonwealth of Nations, the United States of America, and all countries of the Berne and Universal Copyright Conventions.

All rights are strictly reserved.

It is an infringement of the copyright to give any public performance or reading of this play either in its entirety or in the form of excerpts without the prior consent of the copyright owners. No part of this publication may be transmitted, stored in a retrieval system, or reproduced in any form or by any means, electronic, mechanical, photocopying, manuscript, typescript, recording, or otherwise, without the prior permission of the copyright owners.

SAMUEL FRENCH LTD, 26 SOUTHAMPTON STREET, STRAND, LONDON, WC2E 7JE, or their authorized agents, issue licences to amateurs to give performances of this play on payment of a fee. **The fee must be paid and the licence obtained before a performance is given.**

Licences are issued subject to the understanding that it shall be made clear in all advertising matter that the audience will witness an amateur performance; and that the names of the authors of the plays shall be included in all announcements and on all programmes.

The royalty fee indicated below is subject to contract and subject to variation at the sole discretion of Samuel French Ltd.

> Basic fee for each and every
>   performance by amateurs   Code E
>   in the British Isles

In theatres or halls seating 600 or more the fee will be subject to negotiation.

In territories overseas the fee quoted above may not apply. Application must be made to our local authorized agents, or if there is no such agent, to Samuel French Ltd, London.

ISBN 0 573 06410 5

MADE AND PRINTED IN GREAT BRITAIN BY
LATIMER TREND & COMPANY LTD PLYMOUTH

MADE IN ENGLAND

PREFACE

Of all our national forms of entertainment, the Pantomime is perhaps the most traditional and shows least signs of waning popularity. The average "run" of the professional pantomime is certainly as long as ever, and for many years it has been a source of considerable enjoyment and profit among amateur societies.

It is for this latter field of activity that this series of "BASIC PANTOMIMES" has been specially designed, both as regards the "scripts", the settings, and the general production problems which face every company in work of this type.

Apart from the time-honoured stories on which all our pantomimes are (rightly) based, much of their success depends on topical, local and current humour, and by no means least upon the songs and choruses of the time— even of the year.

With this in view, these "basic" pantomimes have been prepared, not as the final, unalterable show, but as *bases* upon which may be built the ultimate product according to the desires, and the resources, of the individual company.

The scripts follow, in each case, the traditional stories very strictly. Any major departure would be resented by the youngest—and the oldest!—members of the audience. The dialogue is in modern prose, and prepared so that "cuts", additions, and the introduction of "local" or "topical" references may be effected with a minimum of difficulty.

Although simplicity has been the prior aim with regard to the settings, these can be still farther simplified where the exigencies of the theatre are exceptionally limited. Alternatively for those who are more fortunately placed considerable elaboration is possible.

Equal consideration has been given to the matter of Musical Numbers, Dances, etc. Those indicated represent what may be regarded as a reasonable minimum; in fact, where resources are available, one or two extra numbers might be added with advantage. But the basic form which the pantomimes take render these additions quite easy to effect.

On the other hand, it will be found that, if desired, the pantomimes may be produced without alteration in any department despite the title of "BASIC", which has, for the foregoing reasons, been conferred upon them.

CHARACTERS

BEAUTY
BENJAMIN BOUNTIFUL (her father)
JEMIMA ⎫
JOY   ⎬ (her sisters)
BATTY (a butler)
FROU-FROU (a dancing mistress)
MARMADUKE
PRINCE FERDINAND (the BEAST)
MATTHEW (his valet)

*(Chorus of Servants, Guests, Farmworkers and Fairies
of the White Rose)*

SCENES

ACT I

ACT II

ACT III

MUSICAL NUMBERS

ACT I

SCENE 1

1	Opening Number. Duet and Chorus	BATTY, FROU-FROU and SERVANTS
2	Quartette	BEAUTY, BEN, JEMINA and JOY
3	Song and Dance	FROU-FROU
4	Song and Chorus	BEAUTY and GUESTS
5	Duet	BEAUTY and BEN
6	Chorus and Dance	The COMPANY

INTERLUDE

7	Comedy Number	JEMIMA and DANCING GIRLS

SCENE 2

8	Song	BEAUTY
9	Song	JEMIMA
10	Duet and Dance	MARMADUKE and FROU-FROU
11	Chorus of Farewell	The COMPANY

INTERLUDE

SCENE 3

12	Ensemble	GARDENERS' CHORUS
13	Ballet	FAIRIES
14	Song	BEN
15	Song	BEAST

ACT II

SCENE 1

16	Song	JEMIMA
17	Song	BEAUTY
17a	Reprise Refrain of 17	BEAUTY
18	Ensemble	The CHORUS

SCENE 2

19	Ensemble, "Lady Beauty"	BEAUTY, MATTHEW and SERVANTS
20	Duet	BEAUTY and BEN
21	Song	BEAUTY, with Ballet of FAIRIES

SCENE 3

22	Flower Song	BEAUTY and MAIDENS
23	Duet	BEAUTY and the BEAST
24	Duet, "The Hikers of England"	JEMIMA and BATTY
24a	Reprise of No. 23	BEAUTY and the BEAST
25	Song	The BEAST

ACT III

SCENE 1

26	Opening Number	FROU-FROU and CHORUS
27	Duet	JEMIMA and BATTY
28	Song	BEAUTY and FULL COMPANY

SCENE 2

29	Duet	BEAUTY and PRINCE
30	Grand Finale	FULL COMPANY

MUSICAL NUMBERS

The following statement concerning the use of music is printed here on behalf of the Performing Right Society Ltd, by whom it was supplied

The permission of the owner of the performing right in copyright music must be obtained before any public performance may be given, whether in conjunction with a play or sketch or otherwise, and this permission is just as necessary for amateur performances as for professional. The majority of copyright musical works (other than oratorios, musical plays and similar dramatico-musical works) are controlled in the British Empire by the Performing Right Society Ltd, Copyright House, 29–33 Berners Street, London W1.

The Society's practice is to issue licences authorizing the use of its repertoire to the proprietors of premises at which music is publicly performed, or, alternatively, to the organizers of musical entertainments, but the Society does not require payment of fees by performers as such. Producers or promoters of plays, sketches, etc., at which music is to be performed, during or after the play or sketch, should ascertain whether the premises at which their performances are to be given are covered by a licence issued by the Society, and if they are not, should make application to the Society for particulars as to the fee payable.

BEAUTY AND THE BEAST

ACT I

Scene i

Scene—*A room in the house of* Benjamin Bountiful.
Up c *is an arch with drapes each side of it. Arch wings set down* r *and down* l. *The furnishings are as lavish as possible. A table at* rc, *a handsome cabinet, a few chairs, tall vases of flowers, etc.*

When the Curtain *rises* Batty, Frou-Frou *and a number of* Maids *and* Manservants *are on stage setting out glasses, decanters, etc. on the table in preparation for a party.* Batty *is somewhat slow and doddering, an old and privileged retainer.* Frou-Frou *is small and pretty, very flirtatious and gay, and may, if desired, speak with a slight Continental accent.*

No 1   *Opening Number. Duet and Chorus* (Batty, Frou-Frou *and* Servants)

This is followed by a lively dance, led by Frou-Frou, *who whirls* Batty *round against his will.*

Batty (*panting*) You leave me be, you hot-headed hussy! I ain't no flying saucer.

Frou-Frou (*laughing mischievously*) Oh, but I *must* dance! I have tinglings in my toes!

Batty. You can have whistlings in your windpipe for all I care—you're not a-going to lug me round like a performing poodle!

Frou-Frou. Oh, but it's a *pa-a-arty!*

(*She tries to stroke* Batty's *hair, but he dodges, glaring morosely*)

ALL. Yes, it's a party! A party for Beauty!

BATTY. Party it may be, but that ain't no call for such goings-on and gettings-off. I'm a respectable butler, I am.

FROU-FROU (*pirouetting*) I dance my way into your heart, yes, you miserable old man?

(*She snatches a quick kiss and dances away, leaving* BATTY *gasping furiously. There is general laughter.*
JEMIMA *enters up* C. *She is the typical pantomime* DAME, *with exaggerated clothes. She has a belt round her waist from which hangs a number of keys. She comes down* C)

JEMIMA. Now, what's all this flap-fiddling about? Here am I, wearing myself to a shadow with work while the servants play around as if they were in a Government office. (*Shooing them off*) Get along with you, do! Go on— shoo-shoo, Frou-frou! And hands off Batty. I brought him up from the cellar and dusted him specially for this party.

FROU-FROU. Oh, but you forgot to take the cobwebs off!

(*She laughs and exits, still dancing. The* SERVANTS *follow, all laughing.* BATTY *glares at them as they exit*)

BATTY (*darkly*) Frenchified bit of frippery! I'd like to have her to meself for five minutes!

JEMIMA (*tartly*) Well, you won't get the chance! She's Beauty's dancing mistress and don't you forget it!

BATTY. I ain't likely to. Prancin' all over the place like a circus pony!

JEMIMA. Oh, stop blathering, can't you, and *do* something. I've got enough looking after a father and two sisters without nursing you as well.

BATTY. Got a lapful, haven't you? (*Significantly*) Some lap!

JEMIMA. Don't be saucy! I'd sack you on the spot if I could find a suitable spot.

BATTY. Where's old Misery-face, Joy? Why can't *she* help?

JEMIMA. Well, call her—*call her!*

(BATTY *goes* L *and calls*)

BATTY. Miss Joy! Miss Joy! Your old skin and blister wants you!

JEMIMA. Don't be familiar!

(JOY *enters* L. *She completely belies her name. She is tall, thin and elderly, with a permanent scowl on her face and a mouth that droops disagreeably at each corner. She never smiles or shows signs of pleasure. She is overdressed, with too many curls in her hair and too many jewels. She carries a copy of Debrett's "Peerage". She crosses to* C)

JOY. Must you shout in that *common* way, Batty?

BATTY. I wasn't shouting—I was calling. You're nothing to shout *about!*

JOY (*putting up a pair of lorgnettes and looking at Batty*) I am not accustomed to being addressed by menials in that way.

JEMIMA. Well, it's amazing what you can get used to when you try. (*To Batty*) You'd better go and give the gold plate a rub up with Brasso, and ask Beauty to come here, will you?

BATTY. O.K. The last I saw of her she was helping Cook. There she set—shaving the Stilton cheese for to-night, and did it need it!

(BATTY *exits* R)

JOY (*angrily*) I wish you wouldn't allow Beauty to demean herself so. After all, father is very rich and we have servants to do all that.

JEMIMA. Oh, let the poor little kid enjoy herself if she wants to. I used to love shaving that same old Stilton when I was her age! Besides, father doesn't mind.

JOY. Oh, I know he thinks everything Beauty says and does is perfect. Just because she's the youngest he spoils her.

JEMIMA. Well, she's such a pretty kid.

JOY (*jealously*) Oh, you make me tired with all this Beauty worship! You've made a complete fool of her!

(BEAUTY *enters* C. *She is young and very pretty, dressed simply and in good taste—a perfect foil to her elder sisters. She comes down to them slowly*)

BEAUTY. Do you want me, Jemima?

JEMIMA (*smiling tenderly*) Only to remind you to get ready for your party, ducks. We want you to look your best for all the nice young men that are coming.

JOY. And for goodness sake don't even *look* at anyone who's not in Debrett. I can tell you all their pedigrees—I've got them here. (*She puts her book down on the table*)

JEMIMA. Hi—this isn't the Kennel Club! It's Beauty's eighteenth birthday party.

JOY (*snapping*) All the more reason why she should learn the dignity of her position.

BEAUTY (*laughing*) Oh, don't worry about me! I don't intend to marry anyone. I'm going to stay at home with father always.

JEMIMA (*singing loudly*) "Oh, if Mummy hadn't married Daddy, Daddy might have married *me!*"

JOY. Well, if both my sisters persist in lowering the prestige of the family, I intend to be the one to raise it. I shall marry no-one outside the peerage!

JEMIMA. Did you say *Beerage?*

JOY (*furiously*) I shall aim at a title . . .

JEMIMA (*derisively*) And start with a double—double D—the Duke of Dillwater. In other words, our Marmaduke. (*She gives a high-pitched artificial laugh*)

JOY. I refuse to listen to your ill-bred insinuations.

BEAUTY. Oh, do be serious, Jemima. I really mean it when I say I want to stay with the best father a girl ever had.

(BEN *enters* C. *He is a distinguished-looking man with greying hair, dressed quietly and in good taste. He hears Beauty's last words and comes down to her and puts an arm round her shoulders*)

BEN. Ah, my dear child! What a comfort you are!

JOY. Anyone would think she was the only daughter you had! What about me? I uphold the family dignity, don't I?

BEN. Indeed you do, Joy.

JEMIMA (*with mock pathos*) And I'm the "little mother", aren't I?

BEN. Of course you are, Jemima. I have a family to be proud of.

No 2   *Quartette* (BEAUTY, BEN, JEMIMA and JOY)

(*After the Number,* FROU-FROU *enters* L. *She is in a party dress*)

FROU-FROU. Come! Your guests are arriving and you're not dressed!

JEMIMA (*startled*) Eh? What?

FROU-FROU. I mean you haven't changed into your party clothes.

BEAUTY. Oh, we'd better hurry.

BEN. We shan't be long.

(BEN *and* BEAUTY *exit* C)

JOY. Haste is undignified, as the Duchess said when her bustle caught fire.

(JOY *stalks off* C *slowly*)

JEMIMA. I suppose I'd better go and get me diamonds out of the 'fridge.

(JEMIMA *exits* C)

No 3   *Song and Dance* (FROU-FROU)

(MARMADUKE *enters* R. *He is rather a vapid young man, with a permanently vacant expression. He is dressed very foppishly and effeminately. He watches* FROU-FROU *for a moment or two and she plays up to him*)

MARMADUKE. Oh, I say, am I the first awwival? I mean—are you alone?

FROU-FROU (*sidling up to him and vamping*) Yes—*all* alone, Marmaduke darling!

MARMADUKE (*retreating*) I mean—er—where's Beauty?

FROU-FROU (*dashed*) Oh. She's getting ready for the party. Won't *I* do?

MARMADUKE. Do? What for?

FROU-FROU (*wailing*) Oh, you are so stupid! I want to flirt with you . . .

(*She strokes him under the chin and he shivers violently*)

What's the matter? Are you cold?

MARMADUKE. N-n-no! Just t-t-tepid!

FROU-FROU. Then warm up, my pet. This is a party, not an Arctic expedition.

(*Music. The* GUESTS *begin to arrive. They enter in twos from* R *and* L)

Ah, here come the guests! Now we must be gay!

(*She whirls* MARMADUKE *around and leaves him gaping foolishly.*
    BEN *enters* C *and comes down*)

BEN. Welcome to my little girl's party!

(JEMIMA *and* JOY *enter* C, *both bedecked with many jewels, artificial flowers, etc*)

JEMIMA. Bung-ho, folks!

JOY (*bowing stiffly to* R *and* L) I bid you welcome to our ancestral hall.

FROU-FROU. And here is Beauty!

(BEAUTY *enters* C *and comes down*)

ALL (*ad lib*) Many happy returns, Beauty! Happy birthday! (*Etc, etc*)

BEAUTY. Thank you, everybody. I hope you all enjoy my party.

(*The Company groups about her*)

No 4   *Song and Chorus* (BEAUTY and GUESTS)

(*After the Refrain they waltz and all the young men take it in turns to dance with* BEAUTY. *As each one claims her he cries*, "Marry me, Beauty. Please marry me!" *She laughingly whirls away from him into the arms of another.*

Joy *and* Frou-Frou *compete for the attentions of* Marmaduke, *who, in turn, tries to dance with* Beauty. *He is
snatched away at each attempt by* Joy *or* Frou-Frou.

Batty *enters and is waltzed round by* Jemima. Ben
looks on from down R, *smiling.*

*The couples gradually waltz off, leaving the Principals
till last.* Joy *and* Frou-Frou *find themselves in each other's
arms and waltz off furiously.* Marmaduke *at last captures
Beauty*)

Marmaduke (*ecstatically*) Oh, I say! How fwightfully,
tewwibly jolly!

(*He stumbles a few times in sheer embarrassment as*
Beauty *smiles at him, and they waltz off* C, *leaving Ben
alone.*

Ben *is about to follow when a* Servant *enters with a
letter*)

Ben. What is it?

Servant. Sir, this letter has just arrived by special
messenger.

Ben (*taking the letter*) Very well.

(*The* Servant *exits.* Ben *reads the letter, gasps, and sinks
into the chair by the table and drops his head into his hands in
an attitude of despair.*

Beauty *enters quietly* C. *She stands watching her father
for a moment or two, then goes to him and puts an arm on his
shoulders gently*)

Beauty (*softly*) Father dear, is there anything wrong?

(Ben *looks up and smiles sadly*)

Ben. Ah, Beauty child, you mustn't concern yourself
with your old father's troubles. Go and enjoy yourself
with your friends.

Beauty. How can I when I see you unhappy about
something? Won't you tell me what it is?

(Ben *rises with a sigh*)

Ben. I didn't want to tell you or your sisters till the
party was over.

B

BEAUTY. I promise I won't tell the others, but please tell me, so that I can help you.

BEN. I'm afraid even your loving heart couldn't find a way out of this, Beauty, my dear. You see, I've just had this letter telling me there's been a great disaster at sea, and all my ships laden with merchandise are sunk.

BEAUTY (*after a pause*) You mean, you've lost—your money?

BEN. Most of it. My dear, I'm now a very poor man.

BEAUTY (*brightly*) But that doesn't matter. We have each other's love, so we're really the richest people in the world!

BEN. My dear—you're right. But what will Joy and Jemima say?

BEAUTY (*slowly considering*) I don't believe Jemima will mind, but Joy will hate it! She sets so much store by riches.

BEN. We shall have to sell nearly everything and per-haps live in a small cottage.

BEAUTY. Don't worry, dearest. It will be rather fun! We shall learn to appreciate lots of things we've never noticed before. Perhaps even Joy will get used to it in time.

BEN (*sighing*) Perhaps. But I would like to see you girls marry well and have good husbands to look after you.

BEAUTY. I don't want to marry. I'm never going to leave you now.

No 5   Duet (BEAUTY and BEN)

(BEN *draws* Beauty *to him and kisses her. There is the sound of laughter off stage*)

BEN. Here are the others coming back. We'll keep our secret till the party is over, eh, Beauty?

BEAUTY (*softly*) Yes—till the party is over. In the meantime, let's be gay and forget trouble!

(*As the others surge on, calling for* BEAUTY, *she takes her father's hand and leads him into the midst of the crowd.*

BATTY *enters and begins to hand round wine with* JEMIMA *helping him*)

ALL. Beauty! Beauty!

MARMADUKE. We want to toast Beauty.

JOY. No, it's time to toast *me!*

JEMIMA. Oh, you're done brown already! Come on, folks, muscle in!

BATTY. Take your choice—ginger pop or sherbet. You'll be able to say "happy returns" with either.

BEN (*holding his glass aloft*) To Beauty!

ALL (*holding glasses up*) Beauty! Many happy returns! (*Ad lib*)

BEAUTY. Thank you, everyone.

BEN. May you always be as lighthearted as you are today, whatever happens.

BEAUTY (*touching his glass with her own*) Whatever happens . . . (*They exchange a smile*)

No 6   *Chorus and Dance* (The COMPANY)

The TABS *close*

INTERLUDE

No 7   *Comedy Number* (JEMIMA, with DANCING GIRLS)

SCENE 2

SCENE—*The same.*

The room has now an impoverished appearance. Some of the more ornamental furniture has gone and in place of the oak table stands a plain deal kitchen table on which are a pastry board, rolling pin and mixing bowl. There are one or two kitchen chairs and a broom standing against one entrance.

When the TABS *open* BEAUTY *is on stage alone. She is sitting at* L *mending some clothes. She rises and comes* C.

No 8   *Song* (Beauty)

As the Number finishes Ben *enters* c.

Ben. Ah, Beauty, my dear, I'm glad you can still find it in your heart to sing after all our misfortunes.

Beauty. Of course! I'm perfectly happy so long as I'm helping you.

Ben. That's my good girl.

Beauty. Besides, everyone has been so good to us.

Ben. I know. Half the servants refuse to leave. They're taking jobs on the farm so that they can be near us.

Beauty. Isn't that splendid of them!

Ben. It is indeed. It hardly seems possible that it is but a week ago since our fortunes changed. What a lot has happened in so short a time!

(Joy *enters* c. *She looks around discontentedly*)

Joy. I wish you could find something to do to earn some *money*, Father, instead of gossiping to Beauty half the day.

Ben. My dear, I was about to tell you that I have just taken a job on the farm.

Joy. I hope it's something *genteel?*

Ben. There are not many genteel jobs on a farm! No, Joy, I'm an ordinary drover.

Joy (*angrily*) Father! How *could* you? What *will* the countess say?

Beauty. Does it matter? You were just telling father to earn some money.

Joy. I meant some *gentlemanly* occupation—like educating backward earls . . .

(Jemima *enters* r *in time to hear this. She has a string of sausages in one hand and a large lump of pastry in the other*)

Jemima (*as she bustles to the table*) Or ministering to aristocratic hangovers! (*She slaps the pastry and sausages down on the table*)

Joy (*furiously*) Must you be so *low*, Jemima?

Jemima. Yes, I like it! What's the matter with *you?* Somebody hit you on the head with a copy of *Debrett?*

BEN. Joy's upset because I've taken a job as a drover.

BEAUTY. I think it's a good job, don't you, Jemima?

JEMIMA. As far as I'm concerned, ducky, it's the tops. I'm thinking of starting a Bagwash meself. (*She begins to roll pastry*)

JOY. You're disgusting! You forget the family tree!

JEMIMA. No fear! I'm using it to hang the clothes line on.

JOY. Well, *I* refuse to soil my hands by working. I shall marry into a titled family.

JEMIMA. *We* know! Marmaduke! Well, you'd better ask Beauty to hand him over. She's got a surplus.

BEAUTY (*hastily*) Oh, you know I don't want to marry Marmaduke—or anyone else. I must do the dusting. (*She starts to dust the furniture, etc*)

JOY. I don't believe Marmaduke's ever asked you. The heir to a dukedom wants somebody more dignified. (*She draws herself up*)

JEMIMA (*using a sausage as a lorgnette*) Have you met my sister, the Duchess of Dillwater? No? I congratulate you.

(BEAUTY *laughs*)

BEN (*pacifically*) Now, now, girls, no hasty words, please. I want you to marry for love, not for money. (*He takes up the broom and starts sweeping the floor*)

JEMIMA (*looking at Joy*) The chance'd be a fine thing, for love *or* money!

JOY. I couldn't lower myself to marry anyone less than a duke. (*She sits L and does some embroidery, makes up her face, etc*)

JEMIMA (*imitating her*) Oh, deah, deah! Not just a teeny-weeny little baronet? (*She holds up a sausage*) About this size?

No 9   *Song* (JEMIMA)

(*For the Refrain,* BEN *and* BEAUTY *sing with* JEMIMA. JOY *mouths the words silently for a time, then joins in. Then realizing she has actually sung, stops, annoyed with herself.* JEMIMA *works as she sings.* BATTY *enters up* C. *He crosses to* Jemima *and looks at her*)

BATTY. What d'you think you're doing? Making a sausage roll?

JEMIMA. No, I'm making a rissole wriggle!

BEN. Well, Batty, I'm sorry I can't keep you on as our butler.

JOY. Oh, don't worry—he'll soon be engaged elsewhere. I heard the duchess say our butler had loyalty stamped on every feature.

JEMIMA (*peering closely at Batty's face*) Oh, is *that* what it is? I thought it was *something* queer!

BATTY. Well, I've got meself a job—see? Got meself a job!

JOY (*triumphantly*) What did I say?

BEAUTY. What is it, Batty?

BATTY. Chief muck-spreader!

JOY (*shrieking*) Muck-spreader?

BATTY. Yes—MUCK-SPREADER! Nowt wrong wi' that! It's muck-spreadin' season!

JOY. What *will* the duchess say!

BATTY. Duchess be . . .

JEMIMA (*slapping a large wad of pastry over Batty's face*) A-a-a-ah!

(BATTY *yells for help and wrenches at the pastry*)

(*Grabbing at the pastry*) Hi! I want that! (*She retrieves some of it*)

BATTY (*with a good deal left on his face*) Nay! How can I go muck-spreadin' like this?

(BATTY *exits, wailing*)

JEMIMA. Someone's going short of Yorkshire! (*She works vigorously at the pastry, etc*)

BEN. I think, Beauty, we had better go and feed the chickens.

BEAUTY. What fun!

(BEN *and* BEAUTY *move up* C)

JOY. How middle-class!

(MARMADUKE *enters* R)

BEAUTY. Good morning, Marmaduke! We're off to feed the chicks!

MARMADUKE. Oh, are you?

(BEN *and* BEAUTY *exit.* MARMADUKE *starts to follow.* JOY *intercepts him*)

JEMIMA (*displaying her work*) How's that for a sausage toad? I declare this foundation stone well and truly laid! (*She proceeds with her work*)

JOY. Oh, Marmaduke! How too utterly deplorable that you should find us in such sheer *squalor!*

JEMIMA (*slapping the dough and inserting sausages vigorously*) Grovel, grovel, squirm, squirm!

MARMADUKE. Oh, don't mind me—I'll go and help to feed the fowls . . .

JOY (*barring his way*) I simply must apologize to the dear duchess. I really will leave cards this very afternoon . . .

JEMIMA (*like a street-crier as she works*) "Old rags, artificial teeth, sewing machines—bought at the door. Spot cash for worn-out coronets!" (*To Joy*) Hop it, young Joy! You haven't done the beds yet!

JOY. *Really!*

JEMIMA. Yes, really! *Beds!* And after that—the vegetables! (*To Marmaduke*) We're having sausage toad, cabbage and mashed!

JOY (*marching off* R; *furiously*) Oh, how *humiliating!*

(JOY *exits* R)

JEMIMA (*to Marmaduke*) And you can help with the washing-up!

(FROU-FROU *enters* C)

On second thoughts, don't trouble! Hullo, Frou-Frou! No more dancing lessons—we're broke to the wide!

(JEMIMA *exits* R *with pan and dish, singing a line or two of* "Round the Corner")

FROU-FROU. Good morning, Marmaduke!

MARMADUKE. Oh—good morning. I'm just off to feed the chicks . . .

FROU-FROU. That's the wrong way!

MARMADUKE. Eh?

FROU-FROU. I'm the first little chick you have to feed! I've lost a pupil—I want another—and I think you shall be that pupil, yes?

MARMADUKE. But I know how to dance!

FROU-FROU. With your feet, yes! But when you dance with your feet does your heart dance, too? No! That is the only way to dance—and I am the only one to teach you! (*She takes his arm*)

MARMADUKE. Well—er—if you say so!

FROU-FROU. I *do* say so!

No 10   *Duet and Dance* (MARMADUKE and FROU-FROU)

(*She "teaches" him as they sing and dance. As the Number ends* JEMIMA *enters* C *waving a large letter*)

JEMIMA. Look at this! Special delivery of pigeon post!

FROU-FROU. Oh—a letter! Is it for you? A love letter, no—yes?

JEMIMA. A love letter, yes—no!

MARMADUKE. Not for *Beauty?*

(JOY *enters* C *trying to conceal her curiosity in a "well-bred" way*)

JOY. Ah—a letter! It must be the one I'm expecting from the dear Countess Mudbath of Sloshing.

JEMIMA. Well, you can all guess again because it's for father. Call him!

JOY. Let us hope . . .

JEMIMA. CALL HIM!

JOY. Really! (*She goes to the door at* C *and calls in a high, very genteel voice, at the same time simpering at Marmaduke and trying to impress him*) Father! Father, deah! Oh dear, my voice is so *tiny*, I'm afraid it won't carry.

(JEMIMA *bustles over and interrupts*)

JEMIMA. Your voice isn't the only thing that's **tiny.**

Get out, pinhead! (*She pushes Joy aside. Bellowing*) PA! Where are you, me old pot and pan! A letter for yer!

JOY (*to Marmaduke*) Excuse my sister . . .

MARMADUKE. I've heard less noise at a Hunt Ball!

FROU-FROU. Or a W.I. Whist Drive!

(BEN *and* BEAUTY *enter, followed by* BATTY *and a number of* FARMWORKERS)

BATTY. Where's the fire?

FROU-FROU. There's no fire, silly old man. It's a letter for Mr Benjamin Bountiful.

JEMIMA (*handing Ben the letter*) Here it is, Pa. Perhaps you've won the Pools.

BEAUTY. Oh, I wonder where it's from?

BEN. We'll soon see, my dear.

(*He slits the envelope and all crane forward expectantly as he draws out and unfolds a large sheet of paper*)

(*Reading*) Well, well, this is good news, indeed.

BEAUTY. Oh, what is it, Father?

BEN. I am informed that not *all* my ships were sunk in the storm, after all. It seems that one has reached port with all its cargo intact.

JEMIMA. Cheers!

ALL. Hooray!

JOY. Oh, that means we have some money after all.

BEN. Yes, but first I must go to the seaport and sell the goods.

BEAUTY. Oh, Father, I am *so* pleased!

BEN (*smiling at her*) We shall not be as rich as we were before, of course, but . . .

BATTY. Enough to muck along on, eh?

JEMIMA. Oh, you're muck minded!

FROU-FROU. Now Beauty will dance again, yes? (*She pirouettes lightheartedly*)

MARMADUKE. Oh, I say, how *thwilling!*

JOY. I must have some new gowns and jewels. Perhaps we can buy a carriage and pair.

JEMIMA. Steady on!

BEN. Quite right—not quite so fast! We have only

recovered a little so far, but at least I shall bring each of my daughters back a gift. Now what shall they be?

JEMIMA. Well, I need a new kitchen sink, really, but as you're being generous, make it a rope of pearls!

BATTY. Long enough to 'ang yerself!

BEN. Pearls it shall be! And Joy?

JOY. Diamonds—and when I say diamonds I *mean* diamonds!

BATTY. Go on!

BEN. I'll do my best. And now—what about Beauty? (*To Beauty*) What shall I bring for you? Emeralds? Amethysts?

BEAUTY. No, Father, of course not! Just—a white rose.

ALL (*in astonishment*) A white rose?

JOY. How ridiculous!

MARMADUKE. How womantic!

JEMIMA. How like Beauty!

BEN (*rather pleased*) You mean that, Beauty?

BEAUTY. Yes, it's the loveliest thing I can think of.

BEN. And certainly the easiest to get for you! Although —it must be perfect—and it shall be, if I have to search the whole countryside! And now I must be on my way. The sooner I go the sooner I'll be home again! (*He kisses Beauty*)

FARM HAND (*shouting*) Good luck and safe journey to Master Bountiful!

(*General cheers*)

No 11   *Chorus of Farewell*(The COMPANY)

During the singing, BEN *goes around, kissing Jemima and Joy, patting Frou-Frou on the cheek, and shaking hands with Marmaduke, Batty and the Farm Hands until, at the end of the Number—*

the TABS *close*

INTERLUDE

If the Number chosen is suitable, this can be continued in front of the TABS, *full company, with business of seeing* BEN *off, etc. Alternatively, a Reprise of Dancing Lesson Duet for* FROU-FROU *and* MARMADUKE, *with* DANCING GIRLS.

SCENE 3

SCENE—*In the grounds of the* BEAST'S *palace.*
    Up C *is a door leading into the palace. To* R *and* L *of this is a garden wall.* RC *and* LC *are trees and down* R *and* L *are garden foliage wings. A garden seat at* RC. *Down* L *is a white rose bush with some roses in bloom.*

When the TABS *open there are some* GARDENERS *at work, pruning and hoeing.*

No 12   *Ensemble* (GARDENERS' CHORUS)

As this Number ends, MATTHEW *enters from the door up* C. *He is an austere type of man, though kindly. He is dressed quietly and is always dignified.*

MATTHEW. Come, come! It will soon be sunset. You're wasting your time in a frivolous way.

1ST GARDENER. Surely it's not a waste of time to sing in such a beautiful garden!

MATTHEW. Perhaps not, but you know the master is not of such a carefree turn of mind.

2ND GARDENER. What's the matter with him? You'd think he'd be the happiest man in the world living in this lovely place.

MATTHEW. He's the most *unfortunate* man in the world! He lives in a prison of his own choice.

GARDENERS (*ad lib*) Aye, he's a prisoner! More's the pity! We hardly know him! Caught sight of him once, poor gentleman!

1ST GARDENER. He never lets himself be seen if he can help it—only to a few.

MATTHEW. That's as he wishes. Now hurry and finish

your work while there's light. The master is very melancholy today and wishes to walk in the garden alone.

2ND GARDENER. Our work is finished here for today. Come, men, we'll go and leave the poor gentleman in peace.

(*The* GARDENERS *exit* R *and* L, *singing the Refrain of No 12.* MATTHEW *watches them go, then exits up* L. *The light fades a little.*

The FAIRIES *of the* WHITE ROSE *enter down* R *and* L)

No 13   *Ballet* (FAIRIES)

(*After the Ballet they dance off* R *and* L.

A moment later BEN *enters up* R *wearily. He crosses to the seat at* RC *and sinks down as if exhausted. The rose bush* L *is now in shadow*)

BEN. A white rose! That's all Beauty asked for, yet it's as difficult to get as the moon. The pearls and diamonds were easy enough, though costly, I'll admit, but I've ridden many weary miles today and have not seen one white rose. Now I've lost my horse and like as not, the creature is on his way home without me. (*He rises and stretches*) Ah me, it seems I'm always in trouble. (*He comes down* C)

No 14   *Song* (BEN)

(*After the Number, he turns and sees the palace door*)

I wonder what's behind that door? Is it some friendly house where I can beg shelter for the night? But first, I must find a white rose. I can't disappoint Beauty.

(*While he is speaking the lights gradually dim a little more, but a spotlight falls on the white rose bush down* L. *Now* BEN *sees it, suddenly, and springs forward with a cry of pleasure*)

Why, here it is! A white rose at last! Why did I not see it before? Now Beauty shall have her gift! (*He picks a rose from the bush*) Just one perfect bloom!

(*He is gazing at the rose when there is a terrible roar as the doors of the Palace fly open and the* BEAST *appears. He is richly dressed but his head is that of a beast. He also has animal paws, the effect of which may be produced by wearing fur gloves.* BEN *turns in terror*)

BEAST (*approaching Ben ferociously*) Thief! How dare you steal my roses!

BEN. I had no idea they were yours. I didn't think . . .

BEAST (*furiously*) Didn't think! Come—what excuse have you to offer for pilfering these flowers?

BEN (*now recovered a little*) I was about to say I didn't realize this was a private garden. I apologize most humbly.

BEAST. Your apologies will not save your life. Rogue and thief—I shall kill you for this!

BEN (*aghast*) Kill me? Surely the plucking of one flower doesn't deserve death?

BEAST. Anyone who trespasses in my garden must die!

BEN. I beg you to spare my life—for Beauty's sake!

(*The* BEAST *stares at him for a moment*)

BEAST. Beauty? Who is this Beauty?

BEN. She is my youngest child—as lovely as a flower herself.

BEAST. Who are you?

BEN. My name is Benjamin Bountiful. I am a merchant. When I went away I asked my three daughters each to choose a gift from me. The elder ones chose pearls and diamonds, but Beauty chose a simple white rose.

BEAST. So? (*Relenting*) She is fond of flowers then?

BEN. She loves all beautiful things. She is as kind and gentle as she is pretty.

BEAST (*gently*) You have a great love for this beautiful daughter of yours.

BEN (*simply*) We are all in all to each other. If you kill me she will die of a broken heart.

BEAST. No—that must not happen. Such a lovely little lady must have her white rose. (*He paces about in deep thought for a moment or two*) Merchant, I will spare your life on one condition.

BEN. And that is . . . ?

BEAST. That you return to me here within a month and bring with you the first creature who greets you when you reach your home.

BEN (*laughing with relief*) That will be the farmer's dog! I accept your condition, sir!

BEAST. Good! Then take the rose to Beauty and don't forget your promise. (*With emphasis*) The first creature to greet you when you reach your home.

BEN. I shall not forget.

BEAST (*kindly*) You have come a long way. You look tired and ill.

BEN. Yes, I have ridden many miles today but I lost my horse in the forest. Now I must go on foot.

BEAST. No, no, you must accept my hospitality for the night. Tomorrow I will lend you a fresh horse and my servants will see you on your way.

BEN. You are very kind, sir.

BEAST. Not at all. You are very welcome. My palace is just here. (*Calling*) Matthew!

(MATTHEW *enters through the door up* C)

MATTHEW. You called, sir?

BEAST. This gentleman is staying for the night. See that he has all he wants and give him a suite of the best rooms.

MATTHEW (*astonished*) The best rooms, sir?

BEAST. The best rooms of all. Tell the servants.

(MATTHEW *goes to the door and claps his hands. Three or four* SERVANTS *enter. The* BEAST *turns away from them and moves down* LC)

MATTHEW (*to the Servants*) Prepare the best suite for this gentleman and see that he has all he needs. It is the master's wish.

A SERVANT. It shall be done. (*To Ben*) This way, sir.

(BEN *turns to speak to the* BEAST *but sees that he stands with his back to them all, with bowed head.*

BEN *exits with the* SERVANTS. MATTHEW *goes to the* Beast)

MATTHEW. Master, is anything the matter?

BEAST (*agitatedly*) Everything's the matter! Matthew —I nearly killed that man!

MATTHEW. But you didn't, master, and I'm sure you never would.

BEAST. Ah, you're a good and loyal friend, Matthew, but it's in moments like these that I'm afraid! Afraid of the day when the beast in me will conquer and I shall do someone mortal harm.

MATTHEW. No, no! You're too kind and gentle to hurt anyone.

BEAST. But you don't *know* what I am, Matthew! Sometimes the smallest things send me into a terrible rage, like that poor fellow picking a flower just now. It seems to swamp me—make me into a ravening beast! (*He shudders*)

MATTHEW. But the rage so soon passes that you have no time to hurt anyone. And then you're so sorry that you entertain them like a prince and shower gifts on them! (*Gently mocking*) Dear master, what kind of *beast* are you?

BEAST. You're a good fellow, Matthew, and I hope you're right, but I want you always near me. Watch me and guard me and see that I do no harm.

MATTHEW. Master, I am your willing slave.

BEAST. No, not slave, but friend. A good friend is worth all the world. Go now, and see that the servants have done my bidding.

(MATTHEW *exits through the door* c)

No 15   *Song* (BEAST)

(*The Refrain is sung by an offstage* CHORUS, *while the* BEAST *moves to the steps of the palace and sinks down as if asleep.*

During the offstage Refrain the ROSE BALLET *enters and dances in the moonlight*)

As the Number ends—

the CURTAIN *falls*

ACT II

SCENE 1

SCENE—*As Act I, Scene 2.* BENJAMIN BOUNTIFUL'S *house.*

When the CURTAIN *rises* JEMIMA *is on stage alone. She is sweeping vigorously and humming loudly.*

JEMIMA. Oh, 'ow I 'ate 'ousework! (*Imitating* JOY) It's so middle *clauss!* (*She comes down* C)

No 16   *Song* (JEMIMA)

(*At each Refrain the Chorus of* FARMWORKERS *and* SERVANTS *enter* R *and* L *singing, and exit as the Refrain ends. At the final one they go into a burlesque with* JEMIMA.

JOY *enters* C *and watches them in horror as they end the number*)

JOY (*furiously, to* JEMIMA) Have you forgotten your ancient lineage?

JEMIMA (*cheerfully*) No, I left it on the clothes line.

JOY. Oh, you're quite impossible! (*To the Chorus*) Get back to your duties, you!

(*The* CHORUS *exit* R *and* L *singing the Refrain, in which* JEMIMA *joins.* JOY *watches, disgusted*)

I say you're *impossible!*

JEMIMA. Easy on with the airs and graces. You're not the Duchess of Dillwater yet, you know.

JOY (*drawing herself up*) I am Joy Winsome Gay Blessingham-Bountiful—a fact which I never forget!

JEMIMA. Neither do I, but not the way *you* think!

(BEAUTY *enters* C *and comes down* C. *She has an armful of flowers*)

BEAUTY. I'm getting worried about father. It seems so

long since he went away. (*She fills the vases with flowers as the scene proceeds*)

JEMIMA. Not so very, ducks. He had a lot to do, you know.

JOY. I hope it means he's driving a hard bargain. I ought to have gone with him, but I *couldn't* bring myself to have anything to do with *trade*.

JEMIMA (*to Joy*) So I suppose you won't be able to bear to touch any of the money he makes from trade? Oh, *no!*

JOY. I shall take all I can get, from a strict sense of filial duty.

JEMIMA. Filial humbug!

BEAUTY (*intervening*) Oh, please don't quarrel, girls. I shall be so thankful to see father home again, safe and sound, that I don't care if he comes back with nothing at all.

JOY. If he does, *I'll* have something to say, I give you *my* word!

(JOY *exits* L, *flouncing out*)

JEMIMA (*looking after her*) Our little ray of sunshine! Mother's blessing and father's delight! Or do I mean blight?

(JEMIMA *picks up the broom and exits* R)

BEAUTY (*sighing*) I feel there's something wrong. Something warns me of trouble to come. Oh dear, why must we have tears as well as smiles?

No 17   Song (BEAUTY)

(*As the Number is ending* MARMADUKE *enters* R *and stands gazing rapturously at Beauty*)

MARMADUKE (*squeaking ecstatically*) Beauty!

(BEAUTY *turns and sees him*)

BEAUTY. Why, Marmaduke, what's the matter? Are you ill?

MARMADUKE. I've got heart twouble! Vewy badly, Beauty!

C

BEAUTY (*concerned*) Heart trouble? You must see a doctor!

MARMADUKE. No—no, I know the cure.

BEAUTY. What is it?

MARMADUKE (*suddenly very bashful and fidgeting*) You, Beauty! What I'm twying to tell you is, I *love* you! Will you mawwy me? *Do* say you will!

BEAUTY. Oh, *poor* Marmaduke!

MARMADUKE. No, I'm not poor. I could give you everything you want, Beauty. Some day I'll be the Duke of Dillwater.

BEAUTY (*smiling*) Marmaduke, Duke of Dillwater! Oh, dear! (*She starts to giggle and stifles it as she sees* MARMA-DUKE's *reproachful look*)

MARMADUKE. Now you're *laughing* at me!

BEAUTY (*quickly*) No, I'm not really, Marmaduke. I'm very impressed. I'm thinking how a coronet would suit you.

MARMADUKE. Then you *will* mawwy me?

BEAUTY (*gently, after a short pause*) I'm sorry, I can't, Marmaduke dear.

MARMADUKE (*turning away in disappointment*) Then you don't love me!

BEAUTY. I like you very much, but you see, I'm never going to marry anyone.

MARMADUKE. But a pwetty girl like you ought to have dozens of husbands—I mean . . .

BEAUTY. I don't want even one! I want to stay with my father. He'd be so lonely without me.

MARMADUKE. Oh, lucky father! (*Suddenly remembering*) Has he come back yet?

BEAUTY. No, I'm worried about him.

MARMADUKE. Oh, don't *wowwy!* His horse has come home.

BEAUTY. Without him? Oh, Marmaduke! Why didn't you say so before? Father must have had an accident! Please go and look for him.

(*She hustles* MARMADUKE *to* R)

MARMADUKE. Oh! P'waps you're wight. I hadn't thought of that. I'll go and have a sniff wound.

(MARMADUKE *exits* R)

BEAUTY. Oh, I wonder what's happened to father? His horse has never left him before.

No 17a   *Reprise Refrain of No 17* (BEAUTY)

(*As the Number is ending* BEN *enters* L. *He hesitates as he sees Beauty, smiling in admiration, then starts to move forward with hands outstretched in greeting. He checks suddenly as he remembers his promise to the Beast and turns as if to steal out unseen. At the same moment* BEAUTY *turns and sees him and runs to him joyfully*)

BEAUTY. Father! Oh, Father dear!

(BEN *stands with his back to her*)

What is it? You're trembling!

(*She turns him to her and kisses him*)

BEN. Beauty, my child! Oh, *Beauty!*
BEAUTY. Is anything wrong? Marmaduke said your horse came home without you and I was afraid you'd met with an accident.
BEN. No, not an accident, but a very strange adventure.
BEAUTY (*looking closely at him*) But you're sure you're quite well?
BEN (*smiling*) Quite well, my dear, only—a little troubled, perhaps, about a thoughtless promise I have given. But first, let me give you your rose.

(*He takes a small box from his knapsack and gives it to* BEAUTY. *She opens it and takes out the white rose which she holds up with a cry of delight*)

BEAUTY. Oh, Father, it's beautiful! I've never seen such a perfect bloom before!

(JEMIMA *and* JOY *enter* C *as* BEAUTY *is admiring her rose*)

JEMIMA. Why, here's the old man back! Wotcher, Pop!

BEN. Ah, my dear girls, I hope all has been well during my absence?

JOY. Of course it has. *I've* seen to that. Have you brought us back our presents?

BEAUTY. Oh, look, Joy! Look, Jemima! Isn't this a lovely rose father has brought me?

JEMIMA. Almost as pretty as the girl who's holding it.

JOY (*sharply*) What rubbish you talk, Jemima. Now, Father, my diamonds, please!

(BEN *has brought out two more boxes and gives one to each of them*)

BEN. I kept my promise. Pearls for Jemima and diamonds for Joy.

(JEMIMA *and* JOY *each open their box*)

JEMIMA. Coo! That'll make the duchess swallow her soup the wrong way! (*She puts the pearls on and preens*)

BEAUTY. Oh, they're lovely, Jemima.

(JOY *has taken a diamond brooch out of her box and is examining it critically*)

JOY. Are you sure they're real? I could have done with something a little bigger, more like the Countess of Crankshaft's.

BEN. They're quite genuine and the biggest I could get, my dear.

BEAUTY. It's a beautiful brooch, Joy. I'm sure it will outshine everyone else's in the county.

(BATTY *enters* L. *He stops as he sees* BEN)

BATTY. Oh, you're back, are you? Gallivanting and cavorting all over the countryside at your age! Got any money?

BEN. Enough to buy us all a little comfort.

(JEMIMA *struts in front of Batty and puts on an exaggerated aristocratic accent*)

JEMIMA. Well, Battay, my man, what d'you think? (*She pats the pearls*)

Batty (*taking a closer look*)   Yer neck's dirty. Try bath-brick.

Joy. Insolent fellow! He knows we always use pumice.

(Frou-Frou *runs in gaily from* l)

Frou-Frou (*squealing*) Oh, you dear, *dear* man! So your horse did not kill you and leave you in the forest to die?

Ben (*smiling*)   By no means!

Beauty. Look at my present, Frou-Frou, my lovely white rose!

(Frou-Frou *goes to her and admires the rose*)

Frou-Frou. It's beautiful! You must wear it and keep it alive always.

(Marmaduke *enters* r. *He is limping*)

Ben. Why, Marmaduke, what's the matter?

Marmaduke. I twied to make your horse find you and it kicked me between the dining-woom and kitchen.

Beauty. Oh, Marmaduke, I'm so sorry.

Batty. Can't you even 'andle a norse?

(Farmworkers *run on* r *and* l)

All (*ad lib*) Welcome home, Mr Bountiful! We're glad you're back! How did you get on? (*Etc*)

Ben. Thank you, boys and girls. It's wonderful to get such a welcome. I must tell you all my adventures.

Jemima (*closing her eyes and with a gesture*) Not before the children!

Joy. Jemima!

Beauty. Tell us what happened, Father.

All. Yes, tell us what happened.

(Ben *moves a little away from them*)

Ben (*sadly*) Well, I suppose you've all got to know, so I might as well tell it to you now. You see, I lost my way when I was looking for a white rose for Beauty.

Beauty. Oh, Father!

BEN. My horse took fright at the strange surroundings and bolted for home, and I found myself in a beautiful garden. Just at first I didn't realize it was a private garden—I was too tired. Then I saw a bush full of white roses, and I was so delighted that I had found what I wanted at last. But when I picked one a terrible thing happened . . .

ALL (*moving forward a little excitedly*) Yes—yes? *What happened?*

BEN. A dreadful looking Beast sprang out on me and threatened to kill me for stealing the rose.

BEAUTY. Oh, Father!

JOY. All because of *you!*

JEMIMA. And how did you get away, may I ask?

BEN. Well, he wasn't a bad sort of Beast, really. He made me stay the night and lent me a horse. But then . . . (*He breaks off*)

JEMIMA. Well?

JOY. Well?

BEAUTY. Yes, Father?

BEN. He only spared my life on one condition.

BATTY. I know them conditions!

BEAUTY. What was it?

BEN. He made me promise, if he let me go, that I would return to him bringing with me the first creature to greet me when I reached home.

(BEAUTY *gives a little gasp*)

MARMADUKE. Poor old Wover!

BEN. No, it wasn't Rover—I hoped it would be—that's why I promised. (*His head droops*)

JEMIMA (*moving in a little; quietly*) Now, what's this —what's this?

(BEAUTY *checks her with a little gesture, and turns to Ben, taking his hand*)

BEAUTY. It was I, Father, wasn't it, who first greeted you?

(BEN *raises his head slowly, looks at her and nods. There are gasps and murmurs among the* CHORUS)

JEMIMA (*in a low voice*) Beauty!

JOY. Beauty? What's wrong with that? She can pack at once!

JEMIMA. Quiet, you!

MARMADUKE. I'll go and fight the cweature!

FROU-FROU (*clinging to him*) Marmaduke—no!

JOY. Beauty must go!

JEMIMA. Beauty will *not*!

BEN. What can I say? What can I do?

(*There is a sympathetic murmur among the* CHORUS)

BEAUTY. Only one thing. You must keep your word. I will go with you—at once.

JEMIMA. Oh, ducks, you *can't*.

BEAUTY. Perhaps he will let me go again, when he sees what we are to each other.

(*She takes* BEN'S *arm. As they move up stage, the* CHORUS *parts into two groups, and begin to sing*)

No 18   *Ensemble* (The CHORUS)

JEMIMA *wipes her eyes with her apron—this business is quite "straight".* BATTY *sits glumly, down stage.* JOY *stands, motionless and triumphant.* FROU-FROU *clings to Marmaduke.* BEAUTY *and* BEN *stand up* C *in attitudes of farewell.*

This is the picture as—

the TABS *close*

As the TABS *close, the* CHORUS *move down and form a group below them, and complete the Number.*

If further time is required for scene change, another Duet may follow between FROU-FROU *and* MARMADUKE.

SCENE 2

SCENE—*The palace gardens.* (*As in Act I, Scene 3*) *Evening.*

The TABS *open to the music of the old Spanish song, "Juanita".*

On the stage are MATTHEW, *at* C, *and the* SERVANTS *grouped.*

No 19   *Ensemble "Lady Beauty"* (BEAUTY, MATTHEW and SERVANTS)

> *The first part of the Number may be sung as a Solo for* MATTHEW *with Refrain for* SERVANTS, *or entirely as an Ensemble.*

Sunset is falling
Moon is rising, mystic, pale.
As lover calling,
Sings the nightingale.
To our garden wending,
Leaving home and love behind,
With night descending
Comes a maiden kind.

Beauty! Lady Beauty!
To our master love shall bind.
Beauty! Lady Beauty!
Here a welcome find.

(BEAUTY *enters* L, *slowly, followed by* BEN. *They move to* C)

BEAUTY.   New life awaiting,
Trembling heart within my breast
Steps hesitating
Come at last to rest.
In your welcome finding
Comfort I did not foresee,
Now my promise binding
Brings no fear to me.

(*She embraces Ben, turns, and curtsies to* MATTHEW, *who bows to her and then turns to the Servants*)

MATTHEW. Bring refreshments for our master's guests without delay. (*To Beauty and Ben*) Pray be seated, sir, and my lady, too.

(*The* SERVANTS *exit* R *and* L, *singing the Refrain which dies away off stage*)

BEN. This is my daughter. Her name is Beauty.
MATTHEW (*bowing*) And if I may say so, a singularly fitting name. (*He holds a chair for Beauty to be seated*)
BEAUTY. Oh, thank you.

(*She sits and* BEN *takes the other chair*)

BEN. This is very kind of you.
MATTHEW. It is my master's command that you are made comfortable and have everything you wish, sir.

(SERVANTS *enter* R *and* L *bearing fruit, wine, etc, which they place before Beauty and Ben on the table and then exit, at a sign from* MATTHEW)

BEAUTY. Oh, this *is* kind of—of . . . (*She hesitates*)
MATTHEW. My master is a very kind and generous man.
BEN. I'm sure he is, and I'd like to thank him.
MATTHEW. I will at once inform him of your arrival.

(MATTHEW *exits* C)

BEAUTY (*to Ben*) This is an extraordinary place, Father. (*She rises and wanders around curiously*)
BEN (*drily*) My dear, it's owned by an extraordinary creature.
BEAUTY (*at* LC) Yet he seems to be so kind and considerate. Those servants are devoted to him.
BEN. You must be prepared for . . . (*He hesitates*) His appearance is a—little startling.
BEAUTY. Perhaps he's not as savage as he looks. I'm glad you kept your promise. We need not stay long. (*She moves to look at the rose bush*)

(BEN *does not answer*)

(*Turning*) I say we need not stay long.
BEN (*not looking at her*) No, dear. (*He rises and joins her*) Then we'll go home together and forget this foolish adventure, shall we?

No 20   *Duet* (BEAUTY and BEN)

(*This should be a "Home" number*)

(*As the Number is ending the lights dim and the door up* C *opens slowly.* BEN *is now at* RC *and* BEAUTY LC. *The music changes for the special music adopted for the entrances of the* BEAST *as he appears in the doorway of the palace. He pauses there for a moment.* BEAUTY *and* BEN *turn and see him.* BEAUTY *gives an involuntary gasp of terror and* BEN *makes a reassuring gesture. The* BEAST *comes down* C *slowly*)

BEAST. Forgive me if I startled you. I was enjoying your singing. (*To Ben*) Is this the lovely daughter you told me about?

BEN. Yes, this is Beauty, my youngest.

(*The* BEAST *bows to* BEAUTY *and she gives a little curtsy*)

BEAST (*to Ben*) I am glad you kept your promise and brought her here within a month.

BEAUTY (*proudly*) My father always keeps his promises, sir. If he gives his word, it is binding.

BEAST (*gravely*) An excellent tribute. (*To Ben*) I see you have a champion in your pretty daughter, Mr Bountiful.

BEN (*smiling*) I have indeed.

BEAST (*sadly*) It must be wonderful to be so loved.

BEAUTY. Oh, but if you love other people, it's bound to be returned.

BEAST. Not always. Few people trouble to look beneath the surface. They're afraid of me.

BEN. Beauty is not afraid, I'm sure.

BEAST (*turning to her*) There's nothing to fear. You will come to no harm here—I shall see to it.

BEAUTY (*hastily*) Oh, but father will be here, too, won't he?

BEAST (*firmly*) No, your father must leave.

BEN. We had thought—a short visit . . .

BEAST (*interrupting*) Your daughter stays—alone. The bargain was your life in return for whoever greeted you first. Do not delude yourself, Mr Bountiful. Now, your daughter belongs to *me*.

BEAUTY (*crying out*) Oh, no—no! Kind beast, let me go!

BEN (*pleading*) I had no idea it meant this!

BEAST. Are you trying to go back on your word?

(BEN *sinks into a chair by the table*)

BEAUTY (*going down in a deep curtsy*) Oh, please let my father stay with me! (*Still in her curtsy, she weeps*)

BEAST (*gently*) No, that cannot be, but there is no need to weep. You will have everything you want here. You will live in a palace and have all the finery a pretty girl has ever dreamed of. You'll never regret it, Beauty.

(BEAUTY *rises from her curtsy and turns away to the rose bush*)

BEAUTY. Oh, how can I help weeping? You're going to keep me a prisoner here—for one little white rose.

BEAST. No, not a prisoner, sweet Beauty—an honoured guest. I won't trouble you with my presence if you find it too—repulsive.

BEAUTY (*turning to him*) Oh, no, no! I didn't mean to hurt your feelings.

BEAST (*turning aside sadly*) It's no matter. I'm just an ugly monster. I've grown used to being regarded with horror and fear. It's my fate. (*He goes to the door up C and turns*) Now I will leave you to say farewell to your father.

(*The* BEAST *exits.* BEAUTY *runs to her father and they embrace*)

BEAUTY. Oh, Father, Father!

BEN. My child, what have I done?

BEAUTY. You're not to blame yourself, Father. I asked you for the white rose. You did not know.

BEN (*shaking his head sadly*) I was foolish. I should never have given such a promise. You must go home and leave me alone to face the Beast, Beauty.

BEAUTY. No, Father! You gave your word and I must

stay. Who knows—one day the Beast may relent, and I shall come home.

BEN. I'd rather die than you should be in danger.

BEAUTY. Somehow, I don't think I am, or ever shall be. Live for the day when we shall be once more together.

BEN. You are my dear, brave girl.

BEAUTY. Go now, Father. Let us say good-bye at once, lest we anger him.

BEN (*embracing her*) Good-bye, my dear.

BEAUTY. Good-bye.

(BEN *crosses to the exit* L. *There he turns and they wave a farewell. Then* BEN *exits.*

The lighting dims a little, except for a pool at C *into which* BEAUTY *moves*)

No 21   *Song* (BEAUTY, with Ballet)

As she sings the Refrain, the Rose Ballet enters and dances above her and to R *and* L. *During this, a spot of light falls on the door up* C *which opens silently.*

The BEAST *stands in the portal, listening sadly, and watching Beauty and the Dancers until—*

the TABS *close*

SCENE 3

SCENE—*The palace gardens (as Scene 2).*

When the TABS *open* BEAUTY *is seen in the garden, gathering flowers. She has a basket of blooms on her arm. A number of* MAIDENS *are with her, also gathering flowers.*

No 22   *Flower Song* (BEAUTY and MAIDENS)

This is followed by a graceful dance. If desired, this may be a ballet, and the MAIDENS *dressed to represent flowers.*

MATTHEW *enters from the door up* C *and the* MAIDENS *run off* R *and* L.

MATTHEW (*to Beauty*) The master presents his compliments, miss, and wants to know if he may speak with you.

BEAUTY (*at* LC) Why, of course, Matthew.

MATTHEW. Very well, miss.

(*He holds open the door up* C *and the* BEAST *enters to his special music.* MATTHEW *exits and closes the door*)

BEAST (*moving down* RC) Ah, Beauty, it was good to hear you singing so happily just now. I must confess I eavesdropped.

BEAUTY. I sing because I *am* happy. You're so good to me, and the time has passed so quickly.

BEAST. It has flown on gilded wings for me. You've given me the first real happiness I've known. (*He moves to the seat at* RC) Come and sit here with me, Beauty.

(BEAUTY *crosses and sits. The* BEAST *sits on her* L)

I see you are no longer afraid of me. Once you used to draw back, frightened, when I asked you to walk or sit with me. Now (*rather bitterly*) I might be almost human.

BEAUTY. Oh, don't talk like that, dear Beast! It's not like you to be bitter.

BEAST. Because you have taught me not to be.

BEAUTY. I don't know what made you like—like *this,* but to me you're one of the kindest and most gentle persons I've ever met.

(*The* BEAST *rises abruptly and walks a little way away from her*)

BEAST (*aside*) I would give all my fortune to be a man at this moment!

BEAUTY. Do you know I look forward to seeing you every day like this! The first time you asked to walk in the garden with me, I must confess I was a little— afraid.

BEAST (*turning back to her*) Yes, I could see you were. But you conquered it. How?

BEAUTY. It was you who helped me with your courtesy and understanding.

BEAST (*going back to the seat and sitting*) And then we began to talk and found we had many things in common. (*He looks at her*) Didn't we?

BEAUTY. Yes, we both love this beautiful garden, the trees and flowers, the music of the birds—the blessing of the sun, the wind and the rain.

BEAST. Yes, and I more than you, the kind, gentle light of the stars and the moon to veil my hideous form. Had it not been for these things I should have gone mad long ago.

BEAUTY (*softly*) But I am now—your friend. Let me help you to bear it.

BEAST (*leaning forward eagerly*) Do you really mean that, Beauty?

BEAUTY. Yes, you know I would do *anything* to help you.

BEAST. Then, Beauty dear, will you marry me?

(BEAUTY *draws back sharply, then tries to conceal her feelings*)

BEAUTY. Marry you? Oh—I didn't think you meant that.

BEAST (*rising and moving to* C) No—why should you? I was too presumptuous. (*He turns*) I didn't mean to upset you, Beauty.

BEAUTY (*rising and moving to him*) No, no! It's just that I—I don't want to marry *anybody*.

BEAST. I see.

BEAUTY. But I'll always stay with you.

No 23   *Duet* (BEAUTY and the BEAST)

(*They exit. Music. Suggested: "Teddy Bears' Picnic". Then* BATTY *enters* L *followed by* JEMIMA. *They are heavily disguised as hikers, wearing shorts, loud-pattern shirts, large boots and woollen socks, dark glasses and eye-shades. Each has an outsize haversack and a heavy stick. They try to walk stealthily. Then* JEMIMA *trips and falls on top of* BATTY)

BATTY. Hi! Help! Fetch the ten-ton crane! I can't breathe! I say I can't breathe!

JEMIMA. Who wants you to breathe? (*She manages to get up*) All right—all right! Don't squeal so! (*Peering about*) I can't see a thing in this fog! (*She pulls Batty up*)

BATTY. You need vitamins! Eat more carrots and other natural foods!

JEMIMA. Don't be personal!

BATTY. You women can never take an hint—I say you women can never . . .

JEMIMA. ALL RIGHT! (*She takes off her dark glasses and looks around*) That's better! I wonder if this is the place Beauty came to? It looks like a posh garden, don't it?

BATTY. What did you expect? A Municipal Car Park?

JEMIMA. Well, I thought it might be more like—(*local gag*) Coo! There's a door! Shall we ring the bell and run away?

BATTY. Wait a minute—wait a minute. Let's get our breff back.

JEMIMA. Our breff back? Whaffor?

BATTY. This is where we have to sing.

JEMIMA. WE have to? Why?

BATTY. The producer said so.

JEMIMA. You're sure you aren't mistaken?

BATTY. I'm never mistaken—I say I'm never mis——

JEMIMA. ALL RIGHT! (*Waggling her stick*) I'll have a word with that producer at the close of the performance. There'll be a BACK STAGE FRACAS! Sing indeed!

BATTY. Why not? (*Pointing to the Audience*) They've paid to suffer—let 'em suffer—I say, let 'em suffer . . .

JEMIMA. ALL RIGHT! In any Repeating Competition I'd back you against any bunch of radishes I ever met! (*To the Orchestra*) A few bars of prelude, pianoissimo, gradually working up to . . . We start at letter "F", half way down page forty-nine. Thenkyew.

No 24   *Duet "The Hikers of England"* (JEMIMA and BATTY)

(*Air: "Marching Through Georgia"*)

JEMIMA. Hoist the good old haversack
BATTY.   And bung it full of lunch,
JEMIMA. Walking stick, and "polo neck"

BATTY.   All gathered in a bunch.
BOTH.   Yell a raucous anthem as our boots the
                meadows crunch—
           WE ARE THE HIKERS OF ENGLAND!

Refrain

BOTH.   We hike!—We hike!
           We 'ike in every limb!
           We hike!—We hike!
           To keep our figures slim!
           Kid ourselves we're happy though we look a
                trifle grim!
           WE ARE THE HIKERS OF ENGLAND!

BATTY.   Don the skin-tight cotton shorts
JEMIMA.   Well up above the knee!
BATTY.   Never mind the goose-flesh
JEMIMA.   There is no-one there to see!
BOTH.   What did Mister Gladstone say in eighteen-
                eighty-three?
           WE ARE THE HIKERS OF ENGLAND!

Refrain

BOTH.   We hike!—We hike!
           This hiking is a hoax!
           We hike!—We hike!
           A pair of silly mokes!
BATTY.   Why were we born imbeciles?
JEMIMA.   And not like other folks?
BOTH.   WE ARE THE HIKERS OF ENGLAND!

JEMIMA.   Climb the steepest hill you know
BATTY.   And down the other side!
JEMIMA.   Over crags and into bogs
BATTY.   You slither and you slide!
BOTH. If we'd known what this was like we sooner
                would have died
           THAN LIVE AS THE HIKERS OF ENGLAND!

Refrain (*During this, they wilt, stagger, and sink to the ground*)

BOTH.   We hike!—We hike!
BATTY.   Oh, heck, we'll hike no more!
BOTH.   We'd like!—To hike!
JEMIMA.   No further than the floor!
          Even that reminds us that
BATTY.   Our sit-upons are sore—
BOTH.   THROUGH BEING THE HIKERS OF ENGLAND!

(*They rise, with renewed vigour and sing fortissimo*)

BOTH.   We hike!—We hike!
          We 'ike in every limb!
          We hike!—We hike!
          It makes us tough and trim!
BATTY.   What would England be without darn fools
              like her
JEMIMA.   And 'im?
BOTH.   HAIL TO THE HIKERS OF ENGLAND!

JEMIMA. Now let's ring the bell and NOT run away! When they come to the door, I'll be ever so perlite like Mum said I was to be, and ask if they'll buy a ticket for the Hikers' Coach Trip to Little Waddling!

BATTY. Oh, you wouldn't—*would* you?

JEMIMA. Ooooh, I *would!*

BATTY. Well, go on—I *dare* you!

JEMIMA (*with bravado*) All right, I never refuse a "dare"! (*Bracing herself*) Up, the Slug Watchers! Hurrah for St Marian's!

(*She marches up to the door and knocks several times. There is a tremendous roar from within and she and* BATTY *scuttle for cover and hide one behind each tree at* R *and* L)

BATTY (*peering out*) W-what d'you think that was?

JEMIMA. M-m-mice!

BATTY. Well, go and knock again. I'll wait here.

JEMIMA (*schoolgirlishly*) You go. It's your turn. Go on! (*Chanting*) Cowardy, cowardy, custard!

BATTY (*coming out* C) Ho, coward, am I? I'll soon show *you* who's scared!

D

(*He marches up to the door uncertainly, with his knees wobbling. He knocks once and jumps back. There is a howling of wind and a roll of thunder.* BATTY *rushes to the tree at* LC *where* JEMIMA *is and they cling to each other*)

JEMIMA (*shivering*) There's a d-d-deep d-d-depression approaching off Iceland! (*To Batty*) S-stop sh-shivering! Who's s-scared now, you big goof?

BATTY (*indignantly*) I'm n-n-not!

JEMIMA. You are!

BATTY. I'm *n-n-not!*

JEMIMA (*shouting him down*) You are—are—ARE!

(*While they are arguing the door opens and* BEAUTY *enters. She comes down to* LC *and sees Jemima and Batty*)

BEAUTY (*surprised*) Jemima! Batty! How did you get here?

JEMIMA. We hiked it—all the way on the back of a milk lorry.

(JEMIMA *and* BATTY *emerge from behind the tree*)

BATTY (*to Beauty*) So you're still sound in wind and limb? I say you're still . . .

JEMIMA. Stop it!

BEAUTY. Of course I am. I'm very well and happy.

JEMIMA. That's good. That's what we wanted to know, really.

BEAUTY. Well, it's very sweet of you to come all this way to see me. How are they all at home?

JEMIMA. Oh, the whole place is love-sick. Joy's hopping mad because Frou-Frou's sweet on Marmaduke, and Marmaduke, bless him, remains faithful to you. Won't look at another girl.

BATTY. And we've finished muck-spreadin' and started compost cartin'. We've lifted the potatoes, put down the apples and put the celery to bed. I say we've put the . . .

JEMIMA. She heard!

BEAUTY. But how is Father?

JEMIMA. He seems to be fretting somethink 'orrible.

Thinks old King Kong's had you for dinner by this time.

BEAUTY (*laughing*) Oh, how absurd! Why, the Beast's the kindest, gentlest creature on earth and I know he'd never hurt me.

BATTY. I don't like his burglar alarms.

BEAUTY. Oh, I suppose you were a bit scared. He's rather sensitive about his appearance and likes to know when people call so that he can hide.

JEMIMA. I must have one of those handy when the man calls for the rent.

BATTY (*to Beauty*) H'm—well, we thought it might be a good idea if you came home for a while.

JEMIMA (*quickly*) That's it—just to let father see you're well. He's made himself ill with worrying.

BEAUTY. Oh, poor father! He mustn't be so anxious! I know! I'll ask the Beast if I may go home for a visit.

BATTY. That's right. Tell him you're wanted in the cowshed.

JEMIMA. Get your bonnet on and come straight back with us.

BEAUTY. Oh, I can't do that. I must ask permission first. You go home and tell father I'm quite all right and I'll follow as soon as I can.

BATTY. All right—if that's the best we can do. We'd better 'op it. It doesn't look as if we're going to be asked to tea. I say it doesn't look as if . . .

JEMIMA. Quiet! (*Kissing Beauty*) Well, take care of yourself, ducks, and don't do anything I wouldn't. Do bring us back a stick of rock!

BATTY. Goo'-bye. (*He crosses* L)

(JEMIMA *and* BATTY *move to the exit* L)

BEAUTY (*waving*) Good-bye! It's been lovely seeing you!

JEMIMA. Good-bye!

BATTY. I say . . .

JEMIMA. Come *on!*

(JEMIMA *drags* BATTY *off* L. BEAUTY *comes down* C)

No 24a   *Reprise Refrain of Duet No 23* (BEAUTY and the BEAST)

(*Towards the end of the Refrain the* BEAST *enters by the door* C. *He takes up the Refrain with* BEAUTY *as he joins her*)

BEAUTY. I had a pleasant surprise just now. My sister called to see me.

BEAST. Your sister? Why did she come?

BEAUTY. She came to tell me that my father is ill and worried about me.

BEAST. He has no need to worry. You should tell her that.

BEAUTY. I did, but she said he longs to see me. Oh, dear friend, please let me go to him, just to reassure him and show him how well and happy I am!

BEAST. I feel I can refuse you nothing, Beauty, but this is a hard thing you ask of me, for a reason I dare not tell you.

BEAUTY. Why not?

BEAST. Because, although I love you, you do not love me. (*He moves away*)

BEAUTY. But I will come back.

BEAST (*turning*) Tell me—will you promise to come back to me within a week?

BEAUTY. Oh, yes, of course I will!

BEAST (*very sadly*) If you do not, then I shall die, Beauty.

BEAUTY (*lightly*) Oh, you mustn't die because of me! Anyway, I won't forget. I'll go and get ready now. (*She turns to exit up* C) Good-bye and thank you, dearest friend.

BEAST (*softly*) Good-bye, sweet Beauty.

(BEAUTY *exits and closes the door. The* BEAST *stands motionless, looking after her*)

Yes, I must die without your love, my dear one. You have captured the heart of this poor, ugly beast so that it cannot live without you. If I were as other men, handsome and gay, I could win your love for myself alone instead of enduring your gentle pity for a creature so repulsive! (*Turning and facing the Audience*) Shall I ever know what it is to be loved?

No 25   *Song* (BEAST)

After the Number, he turns and stands holding out his arms to the door through which Beauty has left him as—

the CURTAIN *falls*

D*

ACT III

Scene 1

Scene—*Outside* Benjamin Bountiful's *house. Afternoon.*

When the Curtain *rises, the* Chorus *of* Farmworkers, *etc, are on stage, with* Frou-Frou, *dressed as a kind of super-milkmaid, at* c.

No 26   *Opening Number* (Frou-Frou and Chorus)

> *At the end of the repeat Refrain, half the* Chorus *exit* r, *and the remainder, with* Frou-Frou, *exit* l.

> Frou-Frou *re-enters immediately and crosses to* c, *meeting* Marmaduke *who enters* r *at the same time. Seeing her,* Marmaduke *staggers, and tries to dash off again* r.

Frou-Frou (*grabbing him*) Marmaduke—come back!

Marmaduke. Wh-what d'you want with me?

Frou-Frou. Can't you guess? It's springtime—tra-la-la springtime!

Marmaduke. But it's not time to spwing at *me!*

Frou-Frou (*drawing him to* c) Oh, *Mar*maduke—don't you love me a teeny bit?

Marmaduke. I can't say I do, weally.

Frou-Frou. Couldn't you *learn* to love me?

Marmaduke. I've never been able to learn anything much! And I don't *want* to learn!

Frou-Frou (*wailing*) Oh, Marmy, what *do* you want?

Marmaduke (*exasperated*) I want *Beauty!*

Frou-Frou (*demurely*) Well, no-one ever called me *plain*—yet. (*She crosses below him and then turns to look at him coquettishly*) Oh, Mar-*mee!* I can't *help* being in love . . .

Marmaduke. Go *away!*

Frou-Frou. With *you*, Marmy—I'd go anywhere with you!

MARMADUKE. Oh, Mater! Mater! What *is* the secwet of my fatal fascination?

(JEMIMA *appears up* C)

JEMIMA. BLOGGO! (*Coming down*) It removes all pimples, cures dandruff, imparts a youthful brilliance to the eye and vigour to the appetite. Advert. Good ar'ternoon.

(JEMIMA *exits* L)

FROU-FROU. Oh, Marmy—marry me, and *I'll* take Bloggo too!

(JOY *appears up* C)

JOY. Hold!

FROU-FROU. Poof!

MARMADUKE. A-a-a-h!

JOY. Girl! How dare you speak like that before the heir to the Dukedom of Dillwater?

FROU-FROU. I don't care if I'm before him or after him—I'll say what I *like!*

JOY. You will not!

FROU-FROU. Yes, I will!

JOY. You will not!

FROU-FROU. Yes, I will!

(*This is repeated ad lib with business until they reach the hair-tearing stage.* MARMADUKE *dances about* LC, *trying to check them*)

MARMADUKE (*during the above*) Oh, please, please, please, *please*, PLEASE! Whoops! (*He has hiccups*)

(*The* GIRLS *stop*)

JOY (*furiously; to Frou-Frou*) Now you've given him hiccups! How inexpressibly common you are! What would the duchess say? What *would* she say?

(JEMIMA *enters* L)

JEMIMA. "Take BLOGGO!" (*Moving to* C) One dose checks this distressing complaint and at the same time corrects any indiscretions of diet . . .

MARMADUKE. Whoops—hic!

FROU-FROU. Oh, poor Marmaduke!

JOY. Be quiet—and don't be vulgar!

JEMIMA. And you pipe down and stop flapping your aristocratic wings like a wheezy windmill! Remember your father's ill—he can't hear himself snore for all this racket out here.

JOY. Pooh!

(*She and* FROU-FROU *tidy their hair, etc, as* MARMADUKE *speaks*)

MARMADUKE. Oh, yes, isn't your father any better?

JEMIMA. No, he's worrying himself to death for fear that Beast has killed Beauty. Something ought to be done!

JOY. Leave her where she is!

FROU-FROU. Someone ought to rescue her!

MARMADUKE. Someone shall! Hic! *I* will wescue her! Hic! I'll hunt for the Beast and wun him thwough with a wapier! Hic! What more can I do than that? (*He dashes* L)

JEMIMA. Take BLOGGO!

(MARMADUKE *exits with a flourish*)

And wait . . . (*She turns back to Joy and Frou-Frou*) There! *Now* he doesn't know!

JOY (*impatiently*) Doesn't know what?

FROU-FROU. Oh, tell us!

(JEMIMA *beckons them mysteriously. They approach her with anxiety*)

JEMIMA (*conspiratorially*) The one-and-threepenny size holds four times as much as the seven-and-sixpenny size . . .

JOY ⎱ (*together; furiously, as they push Jemima*
FROU-FROU ⎰ *aside*) A-a-a-ah!

(*They dash* L *and collide with* BATTY *who enters at that moment*)

Out of our way! (*They throw him aside*)

(Joy *and* Frou-Frou *dash off* l)

Batty (*picking himself up and moving to Jemima*) Hey!
What goes on?

Jemima (*to the Audience*) It is also obtainable in con-
venient tabloid form for teravelling . . . (*She turns to
Batty*) Batty! A duet!

Batty. Why?

Jemima.   Ours not to reason why,
                  Ours but to do what it sy!
                  Into the orchestra well,
                  Rose the conductor!

(*To the Conductor*) What-cher, George! They've let you
out again I see!

Batty (*to the Conductor*) How do? What's it like at the
Scrubbs these days?

Conductor. That is quite sufficient.

No 27   Duet (Jemima and Batty)

(Jemima *and* Batty *exit* r.
Joy *enters* l *followed by* Frou-Frou)

Joy (*moving to* lc) Too late! Too late! I must follow
him! There's no time to be lost!

Frou Frou. I shall go too!

Joy. You will not!

Frou-Frou. Yes, I shall!

Joy. You will not!

Frou-Frou. Yes, I shall . . . Ah! What is that?

(*Shouts of excitement, etc, heard off* r. Jemima *rushes in,
followed by* Batty)

Jemima. Hooray! Beauty's come back!

Joy. No!

Batty. Yes, she have!

Frou-Frou. How lovely!

(Ben *rushes in up* c)

Ben. Jemima! Joy! Batty! Beauty—Beauty's come
back! I saw it out of my window . . .

Jemima. O.K. Take it easy, Pop!

BATTY (*dashing up to the exit* C *and looking off* R) Here they are!

(*He returns to* RC *as the* CHORUS *enters up* C *and at* R, *laughing and cheering. When half the* CHORUS *is on*, BEAUTY *enters and the rest follow. She moves down and* BEN *goes to her at* C *as the* CHORUS *forms a complete stage picture*)

BEN. Beauty! Beauty, my child! I can hardly believe it is really you!
BEAUTY. Father, dear!

(*They embrace.* JEMIMA *and* BATTY *both sniff and sob, with handkerchiefs out. This is done to break the tension, not in ridicule*)

JOY. What an ill-bred display of emotion! What would the . . .
JEMIMA. Shurrup, you!
BEAUTY. But, Father, you look quite ill! What have you been doing? Haven't they been looking after you?
JEMIMA. I beg yours? Not a month has gone by without him having an egg. Being on a farm, we get twelve per year, per pot per person!
BEAUTY. Oh, I know! But what have you been up to, Father?
BEN. Why, wondering about my little girl, I suppose. And all the time I needn't have been anxious. You look wonderful, my dear.
BEAUTY. The Beast has been kindness itself, and they all do everything they can to make me happy.
JOY. Personally, I'd rather live in the Zoo!
JEMIMA. Personally, I think you ought to!
BEN. Well, well, I'm thankful to hear he has been good to you. I feel better already! And now we can settle down together once more and forget what we've been through.

(*The* CHORUS *cheers*)

FARMWORKER. That's roight! Settle down, loike—an' celebrate wi' a real 'Arvest 'Ome Supper!

(*A slight pause, seeing* BEAUTY *is distressed*)

BEAUTY. But you don't understand! I'm sorry, Father, but I promised the Beast I'd go back to him within a week. I came on that condition.

BEN. It's not fair! He can't keep my child from me like this!

JOY. Why not? You promised him!

JEMIMA. It's not safe—she shan't go back!

BEAUTY. Oh, please! At least, I'll be with you here, and happy, for a week. The future may not be so bad as you suppose.

No 28   *Song* (BEAUTY and FULL COMPANY)

(*After the Number,* BEAUTY *leads* BEN *off up* C, *and the* CHORUS *exits* R *and* L)

BATTY. Now, look here, that's all very pretty, but I reckon we ought to have told her that Marmaduke was off hunting that there Beast.

FROU-FROU. We certainly should!

JOY. Why? If she knew, she'd be off again like a shot. She ought to stay and look after father.

JEMIMA (*to Joy*) Now, what's in *your* mind, Soapy Sal? I think I have it! You want Beauty to overstay her leave, then go back and be knocked off by the Beast. Nothing doing! I say—let's all follow Marmaduke, capture the Beast, and make him let Beauty off for ever! Hunt the Beast!

FROU-FROU. Yes! Yes! That's right!

(CHORUS *cheer. Ad lib:* "The hunt! To the hunt!")

JOY. No!

FROU-FROU. YES! And when we bring Marmaduke back safe and sound, I marry him!

JOY. No, you won't!

FROU-FROU. Yes, I will!

JOY. No, you won't!

FROU-FROU. Yes, I will!

JEMIMA
BATTY } (*together*) STOP IT!

(BEAUTY *appears up* C. *The others do not see her*)

CHORUS (*singing*)
> A-hunting we will go!
> A-hunting we will go!
> Tantivvy, tantivvy, tantivvy,
> A-hunting we will go!

(*The* CHORUS *rushes off shouting,* "Yoicks! Tally-ho!" etc. *The others are about to follow when* BEAUTY *calls to them*)

BEAUTY. Stop! Where are you going?
BATTY. S'cuse me—engagement!

(BATTY *exits*)

JEMIMA. Where are me 'ounds? Where are me 'orses?

(JEMIMA *exits*)

FROU-FROU. To the Hunt—and Marmaduke!

(FROU-FROU *exits*)

BEAUTY (*coming down; to* Joy) Marmaduke? Who—what is he hunting?
JOY. Never mind that. I want a talk with you.
BEAUTY. Oh—what about?
JOY. I think you ought to stay with father longer than a week.
BEAUTY. Do you? Why?
JOY. Because he's much worse than you suppose. If you were to go back too soon he'd probably die.
BEAUTY. Oh surely not!
JOY. It's your duty to stay with him as long as he wants you.

(JOY *exits* R)

BEAUTY (*dubiously*) Oh dear, I suppose the Beast will understand if I stay. I don't want to upset father.

(BEN *enters up* C)

BEN. All alone, Beauty, my dear?

BEAUTY. Yes, father. They've all gone off hunting—
with Marmaduke, and they all seem to have gone mad!

BEN. Never mind, dear. Perhaps they're all excited
over your return and want to celebrate. Perhaps they
think that you and I would like to be alone.

BEAUTY. Dear Father! You've always an excuse for
everybody, haven't you? Well, we are alone now, and
we'll make the most of it.

BEN (*sitting* LC) Indeed, indeed we will!

BEAUTY *begins to sing a Reprise of No 28, completing a
Refrain as—*

the TABS *close*

Suggested INTERLUDE *between scene change, a "hunting"
number by* MARMADUKE *and* CHORUS *of* FARMWORKERS.

SCENE 2

SCENE—*The gardens of the* BEAST'S *palace. Evening.*

When the TABS *open the stage is empty. Soft, distant music is
heard, and the* ROSE FAIRIES *enter from* R *and* L *and dance a
short* BALLET. *As the dancing reaches a close the* BEAST *enters
from the palace door up* C, *wearily, with dragging steps. The*
FAIRIES *gradually cease dancing and pose around him, some
kneeling, and all with arms outstretched in welcome.*

BEAST. Ah, Fairies—Fairies of the Rose, can you
bring my Beauty back to me? A week—two weeks—have
fled, and there is nothing left for me now but to wither
and to die.

(*To very soft music, the* FAIRIES *dance about him, bringing
him down* L *below the rose bush, where he reclines, drawing his
cloak over him. The* FAIRIES *dance away up* R, *retreating,
with gestures of farewell. Then they dance in a close circle, as
if talking to each other, finally dancing off up* L. MATTHEW

*comes on from the palace door, looking about as if searching.
At last he comes down* LC *and sees the Beast*)

MATTHEW. Alas, poor master! Shall I awaken him?
No—it is best he should sleep, and in sleep forget his
sorrow.

(*A hunting horn is heard off* R. MATTHEW *turns and
listens. Then* MARMADUKE *enters with a* CHORUS *of* FARM-
WORKERS *armed with pitchforks, sticks, etc*)

MARMADUKE (*coming to* C) Ah! This must be the place!

(*Murmurs of* "Aye, aye, this must be it! The Beast!
The Beast! Where be 'un?" *etc*)

MATTHEW (*down* LC, *hiding the Beast from their view*)
What would you, sir, and these unruly fellows?

MARMADUKE (*seeing Matthew for the first time*) Ah, tell
me, fellow, does a fewocious Beast live here?

MATTHEW. There is no ferocious beast here—no. And
this is private property.

(*Murmurs rise, and then* FROU-FROU *runs in, followed by*
JOY)

JOY. Your Grace! Your Grace!

FROU-FROU. Ah, darling Marmaduke! We have
caught you up!

MARMADUKE. Good gwacious! This is tewwible! I
cannot have women on safawi!

FROU-FROU. Oh, yes, you can—you can have spag-
hetti on chips as well.

JOY. Don't be common! (*To Marmaduke*) I must
apologize for my attire—I know one should always dress
for dinner in the jungle.

MARMADUKE. There is no place for *women!*

FROU-FROU. That dear little tent will suit me nicely—
how sweet of you, Marmy!

JOY. How dare you! (*To Marmaduke*) I know all about
huntin'! Baron Bluebottle told me I should be a dead
shot.

FROU-FROU. You mean he said you should be shot dead!

JOY. You piffling little prancer!

FROU-FROU. You moth-eaten old snob!

MARMADUKE. Weally, ladies—ladies!

JOY. There is only one lady here!

FROU-FROU. That's me!

MARMADUKE. Be quiet! I'm just asking this man here the whereabouts of the Beast.

MATTHEW. There's no Beast *here*. You want the Dragon of Doomful Downs!

MARMADUKE. Oh, do I?

MATTHEW. Go back the way you came, turn right at the *Skeleton Arms*, walk down Creaking Gallows Lane, over the Haunted Bog, and you'll find him in Gurgling Gulch.

MARMADUKE. Wonderful—eh?

FARMWORKERS (*generally, ad lib*) Come on, master! We'll be with ye! Bain't afraid o' he! (*Etc*)

FROU-FROU. And I'll come, too.

JOY. You will not!

FROU-FROU. Yes, I shall!

MARMADUKE. On! On!

(MARMADUKE *and the* FARMWORKERS *rush off* R, *taking* FROU-FROU *and* JOY *with them, still quarrelling and shouting at each other.* MATTHEW *moves up, watching them off.*

JEMIMA *and* BATTY *enter up* L. MATTHEW *turns*)

JEMIMA. S'cuse me, has the Hunt passed this way?

MATTHEW. They have. I've sent them to Gurgling Gulch to find the Beast.

JEMIMA. Oh, you naughty boy! It's all right—*I* know! We'll go and keep them off the scent, and then come back for a cosy chat! Come on, Batty!

(*She drags* BATTY R)

BATTY. That's the wrong way!

JEMIMA. You're batty, Batty! Come along o' me! (*Dragging him off*) Tally-ho! Tally-ho!

(JEMIMA *and* BATTY *exit*)

MATTHEW (*moving down; to the Beast*) Master! Master! You must awake, and hide!

(BEAUTY *enters up* L *and comes* C *quickly*)

BEAUTY. Matthew! Oh, Matthew!

MATTHEW. Lady Beauty! At last!

BEAUTY. Is he well, Matthew? Is he here?

MATTHEW (*pointing to the Beast*) There, lady, but so ill! So ill!

BEAUTY. O-oh!

MATTHEW. I cannot waken him! And the Hunt is after him!

BEAUTY. The Hunt?

MATTHEW. I have sent them astray, but they will return, I fear.

BEAUTY. Keep them away, Matthew, and leave your master now to me.

MATTHEW. I will, dear lady. I will do my best.

(MATTHEW *exits* R)

BEAUTY (*kneeling by the Beast*) Oh, dear, dear Beast. Waken, and speak to me! It is your Beauty, who has come back to you!

(*The* BEAST *rouses, lifts his head, gazes at her wearily, and then sinks down again*)

(*Agitatedly*) Oh, why did I let Joy persuade me to stay on? It was a cruel trick—I see that now! (*To the Beast*) Oh, speak to me, dear Beastie! Last night I dreamed you wanted me, and then I knew how much I wanted *you*. I've missed you so, say you've missed me, too! I'll never, never leave you so long again!

BEAST (*slowly and sadly*) It's too late, Beauty. You left me and you did not come back at the appointed time. Now I must die.

BEAUTY (*very upset*) Oh, no, no! Don't say that!

BEAST. It's true. I warned you.

BEAUTY (*weeping*) I didn't think you meant it! Oh, I've been so wicked! Don't die, darling Beastie! You mustn't!

BEAST (*gasping*) I cannot help it. There's only one thing left to save me.

BEAUTY. Oh, what is it? I'll do anything to save you—

anything! I love you, my darling Beast—do you hear that?
I *love* you and I want you to marry me, so please don't
die!

(*Dramatic music and* BLACK-OUT. *Then the* LIGHTS *go up
again and a handsome young* PRINCE *is standing at* LC *with*
BEAUTY *at* C, *gazing at him in wonder*)

Oh, who are you?

PRINCE. I am the Beast, whose life you just saved. (*He
moves to her and takes her hands*)

BEAUTY. *You* are my dear Beast? I don't understand.

PRINCE. Many years ago a wicked fairy cast an evil
spell upon me, and I was doomed to remain a beast until
a beautiful girl fell in love with me and promised to
marry me.

BEAUTY (*smiling shyly*) Oh, I see!

PRINCE. The Rose Fairy gave me that white rose bush
to help me break the spell . . .

BEAUTY. And it did! Perhaps the Fairy also prompted
me to ask my father for a white rose on that day!

PRINCE (*softly*) Are you glad, Beauty?

BEAUTY (*turning to him*) So glad that I can hardly
believe it. Glad that I came back in time to save you,
dear dear . . . (*She hesitates*)

PRINCE (*smiling*) My name is Prince Ferdinand.

BEAUTY. Prince Ferdinand of Meltonia? Why, then
you're—you're very rich!

PRINCE. I'm afraid so! Does it matter?

BEAUTY. No, except that I'm very glad I told you I
loved you before I knew. You see, I love you for what you
are, and I would still go on loving you if you turned back
into a beast again.

PRINCE (*embracing her*) Dear Beauty! That's the kind
of love that's life itself! I loved *you* from the very first
moment I saw you, but I daren't tell you so!

BEAUTY. And now we're free to love each other for
ever!

No 29   *Duet* (BEAUTY and PRINCE)

(*When the Number finishes, they embrace.* MARMADUKE

enters R *and sees them in each other's arms. He stands very still and looks downcast. They turn and see him*)

BEAUTY. Marmaduke!

MARMADUKE. Er—excuse me—I'm sowwy to intwwupt, but someone sent me the wrong way. Have you seen a sort of *beast* awound here?

PRINCE. Yes, what do you want with him?

MARMADUKE (*politely*) Well, I thought of killing him.

BEAUTY. You mustn't do that, Marmaduke. I want him.

MARMADUKE. But I'm going to save you fwom his clutches! (*To the Prince*) That is, if you haven't alweady done it, sir.

PRINCE. I have, in a way. You see, I was the Beast.

MARMADUKE (*sadly*) I wonder why nobody ever takes me sewiously.

BEAUTY (*gently*) It's true, Marmaduke. This is Prince Ferdinand, and he was bewitched until I released him.

MARMADUKE. You weleased him? How?

BEAUTY. I fell in love with him and promised to marry him.

MARMADUKE (*blankly*) Oh. (*Pulling himself together*) Then it's a love match for the Pwince. Well—(*holding out his hand to the Prince*) allow me to congwatulate you, your Highness. You've won the pwize, but a Dillwater knows how to get his second wind!

PRINCE (*gravely, shaking hands*) Thanks, Dillwater.

BEAUTY. Thank you, Marmaduke. I hope you'll be as happy as we are one day.

MARMADUKE. Oh, no! I shall *always* be misewable when I think of you.

(FROU-FROU *enters* R *running. She stops short when she sees the others*)

FROU-FROU. Oh, *Mar*maduke! I thought I'd lost you!

MARMADUKE. I wather hoped you had.

PRINCE. Why, who is this pretty little girl? I must introduce her to my Court.

BEAUTY. This is Frou-Frou. She used to teach me

dancing. (*To Frou-Frou*) This is Prince Ferdinand whom I'm going to marry.

(FROU-FROU *curtsies*)

FROU-FROU. Oh, how *romantic!* O-oh, I should *love* to come to your Court, your Highness.

MARMADUKE (*hastily*) No, you can't do that.

FROU-FROU. Why not? It'll be full of the most *gorgeous* men!

MARMADUKE. I know. That's what I'm afwaid of.

BEAUTY. Marmaduke, I believe you're jealous.

FROU-FROU. Oh, *Mar*maduke! (*She flings herself into his arms*)

MARMADUKE (*kissing Frou-Frou*) Oh, we *are* being middle-class, aren't we? I wish the mater could see!

(JEMIMA *and* BATTY *enter* R *talking*)

JEMIMA. We've lost track of everybody now. I told you it was no use baying like a hound. It puts 'em off.

BATTY. What's all this 'ere?

JEMIMA (*pointing to the group at* C) That there? Well, I'll be sozzled!

BEAUTY. Allow me to introduce His Royal Highness, Prince Ferdinand of Meltonia.

JEMIMA. A *Prince!* Well, slosh me with a sceptre!

BATTY. How do, your Royal Highness. If you ever want any muck-spreadin' doin' . . .

MARMADUKE. Don't let the side down, Batty, old boy.

(*The* PRINCE *comes forward and shakes hands with* JEMIMA *and* BATTY)

BEAUTY. This is my sister . . .

(MATTHEW *comes running on* R *chased by* JOY)

JOY (*shrieking delightedly*) I've found one! I've found a man!

(*She catches Matthew and holds him firmly*)

PRINCE. It's Matthew, poor fellow!

(BEN *enters* R)

BEN. Beauty! At last!

(*They embrace.
The* CHORUS *enters shouting*)

ALL. The Beast! The Beast! We want the Beast!

BEAUTY. Oh, quiet—*please!*

BEN (*to Beauty*) Who is this strange young man?

PRINCE (*holding up his hand*) Stop! I will explain to you all.

(*There is silence as all draw near to listen*)

I am the Beast!

(*The* CHORUS *reacts*)

MATTHEW. Master! You!

PRINCE (*smiling*) Yes, Matthew, I have come into my own at last. I was released from that evil spell by the love of a beautiful girl. (*He turns to* BEAUTY *and draws her forward*) Beauty loved me in spite of my ugliness and promised to marry me. It is the old story of goodness and love triumphing over evil once again.

BEAUTY. Allow me to introduce His Royal Highness Prince Ferdinand of Meltonia.

ALL. Hurrah! Hurrah for the Prince!

JOY. A *Prince?* What *would* the duchess say?

(*She collapses into the arms of* MATTHEW)

PRINCE (*to the Crowd*) Thank you. And now, there is one thing more I must do. (*He turns to Ben*) I would ask for the hand of your daughter in marriage, sir.

BEN. Nothing would give me greater pleasure, your Highness. I see you love each other.

FROU-FROU. Oh, *Mar*maduke! How *romantic!* (*She hugs him*)

MARMADUKE. Oh, wather! I mean—what?

JEMIMA (*to Batty*) Oh, I feel so excited! Kiss me, you old curmudgeon!

BATTY. Well, I might as well be poisoned as shot! (*He grabs her and gives her a "caveman" kiss*)

PRINCE. I proclaim a general holiday throughout the

kingdom! Let the joy bells ring and everyone make merry!

ALL (*cheering*) Hooray! Hooray! Long live Prince Ferdinand and Beauty!

(*The* FAIRIES *enter*)

No 30   *Grand Finale* (FULL COMPANY)

CURTAIN

FURNITURE AND PROPERTY PLOT

ACT I

SCENE 1

On stage: Table. *On it:* glasses, decanters, etc
        Cabinet
        Chairs
        Vases of flowers

Off stage: Debrett's *Peerage* (JOY)
        Letter (SERVANT)

Personal: Keys (JEMIMA)
        Lorgnettes (JOY)

SCENE 2

On stage: *Strike:* Some furniture
        Set: kitchen table. *On it:* pastry board, rolling pin,
               mixing bowl, pans, etc
        Chairs
        Broom
        Clothes, mending material, duster, embroidery
           on chairs L

Off stage: Sausages, pastry (JEMIMA)
        Letter (JEMIMA)

SCENE 3

On stage: Seat
        Rose tree

Off stage: Hoes, etc (GARDENERS)

ACT II

SCENE 1

Off stage: Broom (JEMIMA)
Flowers (BEAUTY)
3 boxes, with rose, pearls and diamond brooch (BEN)

SCENE 2

On stage: Chairs
Table

Off stage: Fruit, wine, etc (SERVANTS)

SCENE 3

Off stage: Basket of blooms (BEAUTY)
Haversacks, sticks (BATTY and JEMIMA)

Personal: Dark glasses, eyeshades (BATTY and JEMIMA)

ACT III

SCENE 1

Personal: Handkerchiefs (JEMIMA and BATTY)

SCENE 2

Off stage: Pitchforks, sticks, etc (FARMWORKERS)

Any character costumes or wigs needed in the performance of this play can be hired from CHARLES H. FOX Ltd, 25 Shelton Street, London WC2H 9HX

ACT II

Scene 1

CHARITY, MARJORIE, DINAH
JANET, DORALIA
(DINAH with rose, pearls and diamond brooch) (Ham)

PROPS

Champagne Glasses
Table

DRAPES: Front, white, off. Tassels, off.

Scene 2

VENTURE: Basket of blooms (Beauty)
HAMET: Sword (Betty and Janet)

PAGEANT: Dark shoes eyeshades (Betty and Pamela)

ACT III

Scene 1

VENTURE: Handkerchief (Pamela and Betty)

Scene 2

CHARITY: Tablecloth, clothes, etc. (Stageworkers)

Any Charity costume or wig used for the performance of the play can be hired from Charles H. Fox Ltd., 184 Shaftesbury Avenue, WC2H 8JB.